Book 1
Python Crash Course

By: PG WIZARD BOOKS

&

Book 2
Fortran Crash Course

By: PG WIZARD BOOKS

&

Book 3
Android Crash Course

By: PG WIZARD BOOKS

Book 1

Python Crash Course

By: PG WIZARD BOOKS

Step By Step Guide To Mastering Python Programming!

Python Crash Course: Step By Step Guide To Mastering Python Programming!

Python Crash Course: Step By Step Guide To Mastering Python
Programming!

Table of Contents

Introduction

Chapter 1: Preamble to Python..6

Chapter 2: Basic Syntax...9

Chapter 3: Fundamentals of Python..13

Chapter 4: Learn about Python loops, strings, lists, Tuples, and Dictionary...23

Chapter 5: Insight into Python Functions, Modules and Classes........37

Chapter 6: Exception Handling...36

Conclusion..49

Introduction

Learning a programming language can be a daunting task for many, but the right guidance can be the differentiator and the ultimate deciding factor as to how well you learn the language. Python is an easy to learn, high-level language which supports both structured and object-oriented programming.

This book aims at making the basic fundamentals of the language clear to the programmers. The dynamics of the language have been explained so as to enable developers to learn fine coding skills. Python has readable codes and an easy syntax thus making it simple to learn. It has automatic memory management system along with a comprehensive library that allows the programmers to write programs in a fewer lines of code as compared to other programming languages like C++ and Java.

Learning Python can be your stepping stone in the field of programming since Python methodologies can be used in a broad range of applications.

Lastly, the book is useful both for beginners who want to master this language and the experienced programmers who wish to revisit the basics or want a manual for reference. We would like to thank you for downloading this book and we hope that the book is valuable for its readers.

Chapter 1: Preamble to Python

Python programming language was created by Guido Rossum in 1989. It is an object-oriented, multi-purpose and interactive scripting language. The language has been designed as highly readable. Python has fewer syntactical constructions and uses English keywords frequently. It is considered as a great language for beginners in the programming field.

Features of Python

1. Python provides rich data types and easier to read syntax as compared to other languages.
2. As compared to other programming languages it allows more run-time flexibility.
3. It is a platform independent scripted language with complete access to operating system API's.
4. Python libraries are cross-platform, thus making them compatible with Windows, MacIntosh and Linux.
5. It supports interactive mode that allows snippets of codes to be tested and debugged interactively.
6. It is a portable language and can run of various hardware platforms with same interface.
7. The Python source code can be easily maintained.
8. It provides support and an enhanced structure for big programs than shell scripting.
9. For building large applications, python can be assembled in to byte-code.
10. Python can be effortlessly incorporated with JAVA , C++, C , COBRA and Active X.
11. It can be used for programming video games, various scientific programs and artificial intelligence algorithms.
12. It has automatic memory management system.

Python is a self-sufficient language and consists of many tools and once the programmer becomes aware of their uses then it becomes an easy task for them. The language makes a solid foundation to branch out and learn other programming languages.

Python Crash Course: Step By Step Guide To Mastering Python
Programming!

Installing and Setting Up Python

Python distribution is available for wide range of platforms. It is easy to install and nowadays many Linux and Unix distributions include the latest version of Python. To download and install Python you can visit http://www.python.org/downloads/ and opt for the desired version. Even though version 3 is the latest but still Python 2 is used widely. Once you have downloaded and installed you need to set up the path. To add the Python directory for a particular session in-

Linux /UNIX –

   a) In the csh shell type setenv PATH "$PATH:/usr/local/bin/python" then press Enter.
   b) For Linux, in the bash shell, type export ATH= "$PATH:/usr/local/bin/Python" then press Enter.
   c) Type PATH="$PATH:/usr/local/bin/Python" in the sh or ksh shell and press Enter.
   d) Please note that /usr/local/bin/Python is the path of the Python directory.

Windows-

   a) Type path %path%;C:\Python at the command prompt and press Enter.
   b) The path of Python directory is C:\Python

Running Python

There are three different ways to start Python. Python can be started from DOS, UNIX or any other system that gives you a shell window or a command-line interpreter. You can right away start coding in the interactive interpreter-

```
C: > python #Windows/ DOS
Or
python% #Unix/Linux
or
$python #Unix/Linux
```

A python script can be executed at command line by invoking the interpreter on your application.

IDE – Integrated Development Environment

You can run Python from GUI (Graphical User Interface) environment as well,
provided you have a GUI application on your system that supports Python.

1. IDLE is the very first Unix IDE for Python.
2. For Python, PythonWin is the first Windows interface and is an IDE with a GUI.
3. From the main website the Macintosh version of python along with IDLE and IDE can be downloaded either as BinHex's files or MacBinary.

Make sure the Python environment is set up properly and is working fine so that
you can execute your codes easily. (Python - Environment Setup)

Chapter 2: Basic Syntax

In the previous chapter, we learned how to install and set up Python. This chapter we will discuss the Python Syntax. A set of rules that defines how a program will be written and interpreted is called Syntax.

Let's understand various methods of programming

Interactive Mode Programming

At the command prompt type the below mentioned text and press Enter

print "Hello, Python!"

The output in version 2.4.3 will be *Hello,Python*!. Incase you are using the new version then you will have to use parenthesis along with the print statement–

print ("Goodmorning, Python!");

Script mode programming

The execution of script begins and continues till the script the finished upon invoking the interpreter with script parameter. As soon as the script finishes the interpreter will not be active any more. To understand it better take a look at this simple program.

Python files have extension **.py.** Type the source code *print "Hello, Python!"* in a test.pyf file and try to run the program as - *$ python test.py.* It will generate the following output –

Hello, Python!

Python Crash Course: Step By Step Guide To Mastering Python
Programming!

Now presuming the availability of Python interpreter in /usr/bin directory, run
the program as-

$ chmod +x test.py   # to make the file executable

$ ./test.py

Output will be –

Hello, Python!

Identifies in Python

A name which is used to recognize a variable, class, function, module or other
subject in Python is called as an identifier. An identifier begins with a to z or A to
Z letters or a _ (underscore) which is followed more letters or a zero, digits (0 to
9) and underscores. No punctuation characters like %, $, @ are allowed within
Python identifiers. It is a case dependent language.

a) Class names begin with uppercase letters and all other identifiers begin
with a lowercase letter.
b) An identifier which begins with a single foremost underscore indicates that
it is private.
c) An identifier with two leading underscore denotes a strongly private
identifier.
d) The identifier is a language-defined special name in case it ends with two
trailing underscores.

Reserved Words

There are certain reserved words in Python which cannot be used as variable or a
constant or any other identifier name. All reserved words are in lowercase only.

not	exec	and
or	finally	assert
pass	for	break
print	from	class
raise	global	continue
return	if	def
try	import	del
while	in	elif
with	is	else
yield	lambda	except

Lines and Indentation

In Python, to indicate blocks of code for function and class definitions or flow control, there are no braces. The line indentation denotes the block of codes. In the indentation, the number of spaces is variable, but inside the block same amount of indentation should be done for all statements. Therefore, a block is formed by all the unbroken lines which have been indented with same number of spaces.

Multi-Line Statements

A new line in Python typically marks the end of a statement. However, the use of line continuation character (\) is allowed to denote the line should continue. Example –

Total = goods_one + \

goods_two + \

goods_three + \

The line continuation character is not required for statements contained within brackets ( ), [ ] or { }.

Quotation

In python, all three quotes (' , " or """) are accepted. These indicate string literals provided the same kind of quote begins and closes the string. To cover the string across multiple lines, triple quotes are used.

Comments

The comment in Python begins with a hash (#) sign that is not within the string literal. After the hash all characters up to the end of the physical line form a part of the comment. However, they are ignored by the Python interpreter.

Blank lines

Blank lines are ignored by Python. These are the lines which have just whitespace, probably with a comment.

Multiple Statements on a Single line

On a single line multiple statements are allowed with a semicolon (;) provided that none of the statement starts a new code block.

Suites

In Python, a single code of block made by a cluster of statements is called as suites. The compound statements like if, else, while, def and class need a suite and a header line. The header lines start with statement (including keyword) and a colon denotes the end. They are trailed by one or more lines that make a suite.

Chapter 3: Python Fundamentals

Now that we know the syntax of Python, it is imperative for programmers to understand the python fundamentals. In other words, we would be discussing the basics on which the Python programming is based.

VARIABLES

A reserved memory location where values are stored is known as a variable. Memory space is allocated by the python interpreter and on the basis of data type of a variable it takes decision on what to store in this reserved memory. Hence, in the variables storing of characters, integers, or decimals is possible by assigning them different data types.

How to assign values to variables?

For assigning values to the variables you need to use the equal (=) sign. The left hand side operand denotes the variable name and the right side operand denotes the stored value inside the variable. Example –

counter = 10   (integer assignment)

miles   = 100   (floating point)

name   = "Tom"   (string)

print counter

print miles

print names

In the above example-10, 100 and Tom are the values assigned to counter, miles
and name variables respectively and will give us the result as –

10

100

Tom

Assigning a lone value to numerous variables at the same time is also possible.

Example –

x= y= z= 1

In the above example, with value 1, the integer object is created, and same
memory location is assigned to all three variables. Apart from this multiple
objects can also be assigned to several variables. Like –

x, y, z = 1, 2, "Tom"

Data types

There are many types of data which are reserved in memory such as; age of a
person is defined in numbers, and his address is defined as alphanumeric. To
define the operations possible there are several standard data types which are
used. We are just writing a brief on them as of now and these will be explained in
detail in next chapters .They are –

a) Numbers – As the name suggests numeric values are stored in this data
type. Upon assigning a value to them number objects are created. Various
numerical types that supported by Python are–
(1) Signed integers (int) e.g. – 2, 4, 44 etc.
(2) Long integers (long), they can be depicted in hexadecimal and octal as
well. e.g.- 0122L, -0x19323L etc.
(3) Floating point real values (float) e.g. – 5.0, 2.22, -88.88 etc.
(4) Complex numbers (complex) e.g. – 3e+26j, 45.j etc.

b) Strings –The adjoining set of characters depicted in quotation marks are called strings. Both single and double quotes are allowed in Python. The concatenation operator is represented as plus sign (+) and the repetition operator is represented as (*) asterisk.

c) Lists – These are mainly flexible data types in Python. The items in a list are separated by a comma and are written inside square brackets. The concatenation operator is represented as plus sign (+) and the repetition operator is represented as (*) asterisk.

d) Tuples - It is data type in sequence, similar to lists. A comma separates the number of values contained in tuples and unlike lists they are enclosed in parenthesis. Lists cannot be updated.

e) Dictionary – Dictionaries in Python are hash table types. They function like hashes or associative arrays and consist of key-value pairs. The dictionary keys are typically numbers or strings. The curly braces enclose the dictionaries and by using ([ ]) square brackets values can be accessed and assigned. For example, to create, add and delete entries in dictionary

 # make a phone book:

*phonebook = {'Tom Halter': 665544, *

*'Liza Raymond': 889966, 'Ronald Johnson': 776655, *

'Kim Lee': 443344}

 # add the person 'Mathew Peterson' to the phonebook:

phonebook ['Mathew Peterson'] = 99887766

del phonebook ['Kim Lee']

OPERATORS

The constructs which can manipulate the value of an operand are known as
operators.

Python operators

1. Arithmetic

These operators execute various arithmetic calculations like addition,
subtraction, division, multiplication, exponent, %modulus etc. For
arithmetic calculation, there are various methods in Python like you can
use the eval function, calculate and declare variable, or call functions.

Let us take a simple example –

a = 4

b = 5

print a + b

Output will be "9". Similarly other arithmetic operators like division (/),
multiplication (*), exponent (**) etc. can be used.

2. Comparison

The comparison operator compares the value on either side of the operand
to determine the relation between them. Various comparison operators are
(!=, ==, >, <, <=, >=).

Example – we will compare the value of a to the value of b and print the
result in true or false. Assume value of a =4 which is smaller than b =5.
Now when we print the value as a >b, it actually compares the value of a to
b and since it is incorrect, it returns as false. Similarly you can use other
comparison operators.

3. Assignment

To assign the value of the right operand to the left operand, we use
assignment operators.They are (+, +=, -=, /=, *=, %=, **=, //=). Example-

num1 = 4

num2 =5

print ("Line1 – Value of num1:" , num1)

print ("Line2 – Value of num2:", num2)

Output –

('Line1 –Value of num1:',4)

('Line2 – value of num2:', 5

4. Logical

These operators are used for conditional statements which are true or
false.

AND, OR and NOT are the logical operators in Python

AND – it returns TRUE if both left and right operands are true.

OR – it returns FALSE if either of the operand is true.

NOT – it returns TRUE if operand is false

Example-

x = true

y = false

print ('x and y is', x and y)

print ('x or y is', x or y)

print ('not x is', not x)

The result will be –

('x and y is', False)

('x or y is', True)

('not x is', False)

5. Membership

Inside a sequence such as strings, lists or tuples membership is checked by these operators. These are of two types (in and not in). These operators give result based on the variable present in specified string or sequence.

Example –

We will check whether value of x=3 and y=7 is available in list or not by using membership operators.

x= 3

y =7

list = [1, 2, 3, 4, 5];

if (x in list):

   print "Line 1 – x is available in the given list"

else:

   print "Line 1 – x is not available in the given list"

if (y not in list):

print "Line 2 – y is not available in the given list"

else:

print "Line 2- y is available in the given list"

Result of the above code –

Line 1 – x is available in the given list

Line 2 – y is not available in the given list

6. Identity

Memory locations of two objects are compared by identity operators. They are of two types – is and is not.

is – it returns true if two variables point the same object otherwise false.

is not- it returns false if two variables point the same object, otherwise true.

Example –

x = 10

y = 10

if (x is y):

print "x & y SAME identity"

y = 20

if (x is not y):

print "x & y have DIFFERENT identity"

Following result is generated –

x&y SAME identity

x & y DIFFERENT identity

7. Bitwise

A bitwise operator work on bits and performs bit by bit operation. Python
supports the following Bitwise operators - & Binary AND, | Binary OR, ^
Binary XOR, ~Binary Ones Complement, << Binary Left shift and >>
Binary Right shift.

Operators Precedence

It determines which operator needs to be evaluated first. Precedence of operators
is necessary to avoid ambiguity in values. For example – multiplication has a
higher precedence than addition. Following operators are usedin Python – (**,
~+ -, */ % //, + -, & , ^|, >><<, &, <=<>>=, <> == !=, is is not, in not in , not or
and)

STATEMENTS

Anticipating the conditions that might occur while executing a program and
specifying the actions according to those conditions is called decision making.
The decision structures assess numerous expressions which produce TRUE or
FALSE as a result. You need to determine which action to take and what
statements to execute if the result is TRUE or FALSE otherwise. In Python
programming any non-zero and non-null values are assumed as TRUE, and if it is
either null or zero then it is assumed as FALSE value.

Following types of decision making statements are provided in Python –

1. **if statements** - it contains a Boolean expression followed by one or more statements.

   A logical expression is used to compare the data and decision is made on the basis of comparison result. If Boolean expression evaluates to TRUE, then the block of statement(s) inside the *if* statement is executed. In case it evaluates FALSE, then the first set of code after the end of *if* statement is executed.

   Syntax –

   if expression:

      statement(s)

2. **if....else statements** – In this an *if* statement is followed by an optional *else* statement.If the conditional expression in the *if* statement resolves to FALSE value or 0, the block of code executes in an else statement.

   Syntax –

   if expression:

      statement(s)

   else:

      statement(s)

3. **elif statement** – It permits you to examine multiple expressions for TRUE and carry out a block of code as soon as one of the condition evaluates to TRUE. They are also optional statements and random number of *elif* statements following an *if* can be there.

   Syntax –

   if expression 1:

      statement(s)

   if expression 2:

      statement(s)

21

elif expression3:

statement(s)

else:

statement(s)

4. **nested statements** – When you want to examine a different condition when a condition works out to be true then you can use *nested if* statements. Inside a nested if statement, an *if...elif ... else* inside another *if...elif..else* construct is also possible.

Syntax –

if expression1:

statement(s)

if expression2:

Statement(s)

elif expression3:

statement(s)

else:

statement(s)

elif expression4:

statement(s)

else:

statement(s)

Chapter 4: Learn about Python loops, Strings, Lists, Tuples, and Dictionary

We have already introduced these terms in the previous chapter. Now we will take a look at each one of them in detail so that you can understand their usage in Python programming.

LOOPS

Typically the statements are executed in sequence, but if a situation arises when you are required to execute a block of code many number of times. In Python, a loop statement permits you to execute a statement or a group of statements numerous times. To handle the looping requirement following types of loops are available in Python –

1. **while loop** – this loop repetitively executes a target statement as long as the condition given is true.
   Syntax-

   while expression:

      statement(s)

   Here, it can be a single statement or a block of statements and the condition may be an expression. The loop iterates as long while the condition is true. When the condition becomes false, the program control passes to the line immediately following the loop.

2. **for loop** – these loops have the capability to iterate over items of whichever sequence, like a string or list.
   Syntax-

   for iterating_var in sequence:

      statement(s)

The sequence which contains an expression is evaluated first and then the first item in a sequence is assigned to the *iterating_var*. After this the statement block is executed. All the items in the list are assigned to *iterating_var*, and the statement(s) block is executed until the entire sequence is exhausted.

3. **Infinite loop**– If a condition never becomes FALSE it becomes an infinite loop. The results in a loop that never ends are called as infinite loops. These loops might be useful in client/server programming where server needs to run continuously for the client programs to communicate with it as and when required.

Using else statements with loops

If an else statement is used with for loop, then the else statement is executed when the loop has exhausted iterating the list. When else is used with a while loop, the else statement is executed when the condition becomes false.

Loop Control Statements

The execution from normal sequence is changed with loop control statements. So when execution leaves a scope, all automatic objects that were created in that scope are destroyed. Listed below are the control statements that are supported by Python –

a) **Break statement** – it ends the current loop statement and transfers execution to the statement immediately following the loop. The break statement can be used in both *for* and *while* loops. Most common use of break statement is when some external condition is triggered requiring a quick exit from loop.
   Syntax-

   break

b) **Continue statement** – The control is returned to the beginning of the while loop. The continue statements reject all the remaining statements in the current iteration of the loop and moves the control back to the top of the loop. It can be used for both *for* and *while* loops. Syntax-

continue

c) **Pass statement** – When a statement is required syntactically but you do not want any command or code to execute, we use pass statement. It is a *null* operation and nothing happens on execution.
Syntax –

pass

STRINGS

In python, strings can be created by simply enclosing characters in quotes. The single quotes are treated same as double quotes. It is as easy as assigning value to a variable. Python has a built-in string called as 'str' which has many features. A literal in string can expand into multiple lines but there has to be back slash at the end of each line before the new line is created.

Example –

var 1 = 'Goodmorning World!'

var 2 = ' Python Programming'

How to access values in strings?

A character type is not supported by Python, they are considered as strings of length one, therefore also considered as substring. In order to access substring, the square brackets are used for slicing along with the index or indices.

Example –

var 1 = 'Goodmorning World!'

var 2 = "Python Programming"

print "var1[0]:", var1[0]

print "var2[1:5]:", var2[1:5]

result –

var1[0]: G

var2[1:5]: ytho

Updating Strings

Existing strings can be updated by (re)assigning a variable to another string. The new value can be related to a completely different string altogether or to its previous value.

String operators

There are various string operators, assume variable **a** holds 'Hello' and **b** holds 'World'

Operator	Description	Example
*	Repetition –it prints the character twice.	a*2 will give HelloHello
+	Concatenation- adds value on both sides and gives results	a + b will give Hello World
[:]	Range slice – gives characters from given range.	a[1:4] will give ell

26

[ ]	Slice – gives characters from given index	a[1]will give e
not in	Membership – if a character does not exist in a given string it returns true	M not in a will give 1
in	Membership – if character exists in the given string it returns true	H in a will give 1
r/R	Raw string- it surpasses actual meaning of escape characters	Print r'\n' prints \n and print R'\n' prints \n
%	Format – does string formatting	Read below

String formatting

The string formatting % operator is exclusive to strings and makes up for the bunch of having functions from C's printf family.

Example –

print "My name is %s and weight is %d kg!" % ('Alex', 25)

Result –

My name is Alex and weight is 25kg!

Triple Quotes

A triple quote in Python allows the strings to span in multiple lines which include verbatim TABs, NEWLINEs, and many other special characters. The syntax for triple quotes include three consecutive double or single   quotes.

<u>Changing lower and upper case</u>

In Python, you can change the string to upper case from lower case

str = "this is an example";

print "str.capitalize( ):", str.upper( )

Result –

str.capitalize( ): THIS IS AN EXAMPLE

LISTS

In Python, the fundamental data structure is a sequence. All the elements in a sequence are assigned a number; its index or position. In python, there are six built-in types of sequences and most common are tuples and lists.

Lists are the most flexible data type which can be written as a list of values separated by comma between the square brackets. The items in the list may not be of same type.

Example –

list 1 = ['english', 'french', 1996, 2015];

list2 = [1, 2, 3, 4, 5];

list3 = ["x", "y", "z"]

Just like string indices, list indices also start at 0, and list can be concatenated, sliced and so on.

<u>How to access values in lists?</u>

The square brackets are used for slicing along with the indices or index to get a value at the index.

list 1 = ['english', 'french', 1996, 2015];

list2 = [1, 2, 3, 4, 5, 6, 7];

print "list1[0]:", list1[0]

print "list2[1:5]:", list2[1:5]

Result –

list1[0]: English

list2[1:5]: [2, 3, 4, 5]

Updating Lists

Multiple elements or a single element of lists can be updated by giving the slice on the left-hand side of the assignment operator. It is possible to add elements in a list by using the append( ) method.

Example –

list = ['english', 'french', 1996, 2015];

print "Value available at index 2:"

print list[2]

list[2] = 2016;

print "New value available at index 2:"

print list[2]

Result –

Value available at index 2:

1996

New value available at index 2:

2016

Deleting elements from list

By using either the remove( ) method if you don't know which element to delete
or del statement if you know exactly which element(s) you are deleting you can
delete a list element.

Example –

list = ['english', 'french', 1996, 2015];

print list1

del list1[2];

print "After deleting value at index 2:"

print list 1

Result-

['english', 'french', 1996, 2015]

After deleting value at index 2:

['english', 'french', 2015]

Similar to Strings, lists also react to * and + operators; they mean repetition and concatenation here as well, except that the outcome is a new list, not a string. As the lists are sequences, slicing and indexing also works in a similar manner as in strings.

Python has some built-in list functions –

1. cmp(list1, list2) – it compares elements in each list
2. max(list) - it returns item from the list with maximum value.
3. len(list) – it gives total strength of the list.
4. min(list)- it returns items from the list with minimum value.
5. List(seq) – it converts tuple into list.

List methods –

1. list.append(obj)- it appends object obj to list
2. list.extend(seq) – it appends the contents of seq to list
3. list.count(obj) – it returns count of how many times obj occurs in list.
4. list.insert(index,obj) – it inserts obj into list at offset index.
5. list.index(obj)- it returns the lowest index in the list that obj appears.
6. list.remove(obj) – it removes object from list
7. list.pop(obj=list[-1])- it removes and returns the last obj from list.
8. list.sort([func]) – sorts objects of list, use compare function if given
9. list.reverse( )- it reverses object of list in place.

TUPLES

The series of unchangeable Python objects are called as tuples. They are sequences similar to lists. Unlike lists, you cannot change tuples and they make use of parentheses, on the other hand square brackets are used in lists. You can create tuples by simply separating values with a comma and optionally these values which are separated by comma can be put inside parentheses.

Example –

tup1 = ('english', 'french', 1996, 2015);

tup2 = (1, 2, 3, 4, 5);

tup3= "x", "y", "z";

Two parentheses consisting of nothing; *tup= ( );* denotes an empty tuple.

In order to write tuple that contains single value a comma needs to be included, even though there is barely a single value; *tup1= (45,);*

How to access values in Tuples?

Make use of the square brackets for slicing, besides the index or indices to get the value available at the index.

Example –

tup1 = ('english', 'french', 1996, 2015);

tup2 = (1, 2, 3, 4, 5, 6, 7);

print "tup1[0]:", tup1[0]

print "tup2[1:5]:", tup2[1:5]

result –

tup1[0]: English

tup2[1:5]: [2, 3, 4, 5]

How to update tuples?

Since tuples are unchangeable you cannot change or update the tuple elements values. You can take parts of existing tuple to make new tuples.

Example –

Tup1 = (14, 32.44);

Tup2 = ('xyz', 'abc');

#Below action is not valid for tuples

#tup1[0] =100;

Therefore let's create a new tuple

tup3 = tup1 + tup2;

print tup3

result –

(14, 32.44, 'xyz', 'abc')

Deleting elements in tuples

Individual elements of tuples cannot be removed. However, there is nothing wrong in positioning together one more tuple with the undesired elements discarded. In order to completely remove a tuple, just add **del** statement.

Example –

tup = ('english', 'french', 1996, 2015);

print tup

del tup;

print "After deleting tup:"

print tup

Result –

('english', 'french', 1996, 2015)

After deleting tup:

Traceback (most recent call last):

file "test.py", line 9, in <module>

print tup;

NameError: name 'tup' is not defined

Please note that an exception is raised because after del tup tuple does not exist.

Similar to strings, tuples react to * and + operators; they denote repetition and concatenation here too, but a new tuple is created as a result and not a string. The indexing and slicing in tuples works in a similar way as it works in strings.

Following are the built-in functions of tuples –

1. cmp(tuple1, tuple2) – it compares the elements in each tuple
2. max(tuple) – it returns item from the tuple with maximum value.
3. len(tuple) – it gives the total length of the tuple.
4. tuple(seq)- it converts a list into a tuple.
5. min(tuple) – it returns item from the tuple with minimum value.

PYTHON DICTIONARY

Dictionary values can be of any kind, but the keys must be of an unchangeable data type such as numbers, strings and tuples.

How to access values in Dictionary?

By using the square brackets along with the key to obtain its value dictionary elements can be accessed.

Example –

dict = {'Name': 'Tom', 'Age': 10, 'Class': 'Fifth'}

print "dict['Name']:", dict['Name']

print "dict['Age']:", dict['Age']

Result –

dict['Name']: Tom

dict['Age']: 10

Properties of Dictionary Keys

a) Per key you cannot have more than one entry, i.e. duplicate key is not allowed. The preceding assignment wins when a duplicate key is encountered.

b) Keys should be unchangeable. By this it means that you may utilize numbers, strings or tuples as dictionary keys but something like ['key'] is not allowed.

Built-in dictionary functions-

1. cmp(dict1,dict2) – compares elements in both
2. str(dict)- produces a printable string
3. len(dict) – gives total length of dictionary
4. type(variable) – returns the type of passed variable.

Built-in dictionary methods-

1. dict.clear( ) – removes all elements of dictionary
2. dict.fromkeys( )- creates a new dictionary with keys from seq and values set to value
3. dic.copy( ) – returns a shallow copy of dictionary
4. dict.get(key, default=None) – returns value or default if key not in dictionary.
5. dict.has_key(key) – returns true if key in dictionary*dict*, otherwise false
6. dict.keys( )- returns list of dictionary dict's keys
7. dict.items( ) – returns a list of *dict's* tuple pairs
8. dict.setfedault(key,default=None) – similar to get, but will set dict[key]= default if *key* is not already in dict.
9. dict.values( )- returns list of dictionary *dict's* values.
10. dict.update( )- adds dictionary *dict2's* key-values pair to *dict*

Chapter 5: Insight into Python Functions, Modules and Classes

FUNCTIONS

A block of code that is organized, reusable, and is used to carry out a single, related action is called as a function. The functions provide better modularity for your application and a high degree of code reusing. Python has many built-in functions but creating your own functions is also possible and these are called as *user-defined* functions.

How to define a Function?

In order to give the necessary functionality you can define a function. Here, are some simple rules for defining a function in Python –

1. A function block begins with the keyword def followed by the function name and parentheses (( )).
2. Any arguments or input parameters must be positioned within these parentheses. Parameters can also be defined within these parentheses.
3. Inside every function the block of code starts with a colon and is indented.
4. The statement return [expression] exits a function, optionally passing back an expression to the caller. The return statement with no arguments is the same as return None.
5. The first statement of a function can be an optional statement; the documentation string of the function or *docstring*.

Syntax –

def functionname (parameters):

   "function_doctsring"

   function_suite

   return [expression]

Parameters, by default have a positional behavior and you need to inform them in the similar order as they were defined.

How to call a function?

By defining a function you only give a name to a function, structures the block of code and specify the parameters that are to be included in the function. Once the basic structure of a function is finalized, you can execute it by calling it from the Python prompt directly or from another function.

Example of function printme( ) is as below –

Function definition is here

def printme(str):

    "This prints a passed string into this function"

    print str

    return;

Call the printme function now

printme ("This is first call to user defined function!")

printme ("This is second call to the same function")

Output –

This is first call to user defined function!

This is second call to the same function

In Python, all parameters (arguments) are passed by reference. This means what a parameter refers to inside a function, if you change it, the change gets reflected back in the calling function.

Function Arguments

By using following types of arguments you can call a function –

a) Required arguments –these are the arguments passed to a function in correct positional order. In this the number of arguments in the function call should exactly match with the function definition.

b) Keyword arguments – These are related to function calls. Once keyword argument is used in a function call, the parameter name identifies the arguments to the caller. This allows for skipping of arguments or places them out of order since the keywords given to match the values with parameters is used by the Python interpreter.

c) Default arguments –in the function call if a value is not provided for the argument this argument assumes a default value.

d) Variable-length arguments – While defining a function it may be required to process a function for additional arguments than specified, these are called as variable-length arguments. Unlike default and required arguments, they are not named in the function definition. The variable name that carries the value of all non-keyword variable arguments an asterisk is placed before it. Tuple will remain empty in case there are no extra arguments specified during a function call.

Scope of Variables

In a program, all variables may not be accessible at all locations. This depends on where you have declared a variable. The portion of the program where you can access a particular identifier is determined by the scope of variables. There are two basic scopes –

a) Global – Variables that are defined outside the function body have a global scope. These can be accessed throughout the program body by all functions.

b) Local – Variables that are defined inside the function body have a local scope. These can be accessed only inside a function in which they are declared.

MODULES

Modules help in organizing the code logically. The code becomes easy to use and understand by grouping the related code into module. A Python object with arbitrarily named attributes that can bind and reference is called module. In simple words, module is a file that consists of Python code. It can define variables, functions, and classes.

Example of simple module support.py -

```
def print_func( par ):
    print " Hi:", par
    return
```

Import Statememt

Any Python source file can be used as a module by executing an import statement in some other Python source file.

Syntax –

import module1[, module2[,. . .moduleN]

From import statement

Specific attributes can be imported from a module into the current namespace
with the help of *from import* statements.

Syntax –

from modname import name1[, name2[,. . .nameN]]

From...import * statement

The *from..import*statement* makes the import of all names possible from a
module into the current namespace.

from modname import*

Locating Modules

The module is searched by the Python interpreter in the below mentioned
sequence when a module is imported.

   a) Current directory
   b) In case the module isn't found, the Python looks into every directory in the
       shell variable PYTHONPATH
   c) The default path is checked in Python, if else fails.

The module search path is stored in the system module sys as the
sys.pathvariable. This variable contains the current directory, PYTHONPATH,
and the installation dependent default.

PYTHONPATH – it is an environment variable, which consists of a list of
directories.

Syntax-

For windows -

set PYTHONPATH=c:\python20\lib;

For UNIX-

Python Crash Course: Step By Step Guide To Mastering Python
Programming!

set PYTHONPATH=/usr/local/lib/python

Namespaces and scoping

A namespace is a dictionary of variable names (keys) and their corresponding objects (values)

Variable can be accessed in Python in both local and global namespace. In case a global and local variable has the same name, the global variable is overshadowed by the local variable. All functions have their own local namespace. The same scoping rules are followed by classes as ordinary functions. Whether variables are global or local is a informed guess made by Python. An assumption is made that any variable is local which has been assigned a value in a function. Therefore, for assigning a value to a global variable inside a function, the global statement needs to be used first. The statement *global VarName* tells that VarName is global. Searching the local namespace for the variable is stopped by Python.

The dir( ) function-

It returns a systematic list of strings consisting of the names defined by a module. List consists of all the functions, modules and variables that are defined in a module.

The globals( ) and locals( ) functions-

These functions can be used to return names in the local and local namespaces depending on the location from where they are called. If from inside a function a globals( ) is called, it will return all the names that can be globally accessed from that function. In case locals( ) is called from inside a function, it will return names that can be locally accessed from that function. The return type for both the functions is dictionary. So the names can be extracted using the keys( ) function.

The reload( ) function

The code in the top level portion of a module is executed only once when the module is imported into a script. However, if you want to execute the top level code again, then use the reload( ) function. A previously imported module is imported again by this function.

Syntax –

reload(module_name)

In syntax, *module_name* is the name of the module to be reloaded and not the string consisting of the module name.

CLASSES

As we know that Python is an object-oriented language, therefore using and creating objects and classes is easy. A class is a user-defined model for an object that defines a set of attributes that portray any object of the class. The attributes are the data members and methods, associated via dot notation. Data member is an instance variable or a class variable that holds data related with a class and its objects. The instance variable is a variable that is defined inside a method and belongs to the current instance of a class.

How to create classes?

A new class definition is created by a *class* statement. The name of the class straight away follows the keyword *class* followed by a colon.

class ClassName:

    'Optional class documentation string'

    class_suite

- A class has a documentation string, which can be accessed via
  ClassName._doc_.
- Each component statement that defines class members, functions and data
  attributes exist in the *class_suite*.

How to create instances of class?

Use class name to call the class and pass in no matter what arguments its _init_
method accepts for creating an instance of a class.

How to access attributes?

Dot operator with object need to be used in order to access the object's attributes.

Built-in class attributes

Dot operator can be used to access the built-in attributes–

a) _dict_ - dictionary containing class's namespace
b) _name_ - class name
c) _doc_ - class documentation string or none, if undefined.
d) _bases_ - probably a vacant tuple containing the base classes in the order
of their occurrence in the base class list.
e) _module_ - the module name in which class is defined. This attribute in
interactive mode is "_main_".

Garbage Collection

In Python, to make the memory space free, objects (class instances or built-in)
that are not required are deleted automatically. Garbage collection is a method by
which Python from time to time recovers memory blocks that are no longer in
use. Python's garbage collector runs while the program is being executed and is
triggered when an object's reference count reaches zero. An object's reference

count increases when it is positioned in a container (tuple, list or dictionary) or is assigned a new name. The object's reference count decreases when it is deleted with *del,* its reference goes out of scope or it is reassigned. Python automatically collects when an object's reference count reaches zero.

Class inheritance

A pre-existing class can be used for deriving and creating a new class instead of begining from scratch by listing the parent class after the new class name inside parentheses. The attributes of its parent class are inherited by the child class, and these attributes can be used as if they were defined in the child class. Just like their parent class the derived classes can be declared. Though, after the class name a list of base classes to inherit from is given.

Syntax –

class SubClassName (ParentClass1[, ParentClass2,. . .]):

    'Optional class documentation string'

    class_suite (Python - Environment Setup)

Chapter 6: Exception handling

<u>Exception</u>

An event that interrupts the standard flow of the program's instructions at the time of execution is called as an exception. Typically, when such a situation is encountered by a Python script that it cannot handle, it raises an exception. In other words, an exception is a Python object that depicts an error. When an exception is raised in Python script, it either the exception is handled immediately or it is terminated.

<u>How to handle an exception?</u>

In case you find a suspicious code in a program, then the program can be defended by putting that code in a **try:** block. After this include an **except:**statement followed by a block of code which manages the problem as gracefully as possible.

Syntax –

try:

  You do your operations here;

  ....

except Exception I:

  If there is Exception I, then execute this block.

Except Exception II:

  If there is Exception II, then execute this block.

  ....

else:

If there is no exception then execute this block.

Please note –

- A single try statement can have multiple except statements.
- A generic except clause can also be provided, which manages any exception.
- An else-clause can also be included after except clause(s). If the code in try: block does not raise an exception the code in the else-block is executed.
- A better place for code that does not need the try: block's protection is the else-block.

Except Clause with no exception –all the exceptions that occur are caught by the try-except statement. However, it doesn't make the programmer recognize the root cause of the problem that may occur.

Except clause with multiple exceptions- the same except statement to handle multiple exceptions can be used.

Try-finally clause – The finally: block with try: block can be used. In the finally block you can place any code that must execute, irrespective of the fact that the try-block has raised an exception or not.

Argument of an exception – An argument is a value that gives more information about the problem and an exception can have an argument. You can catch an exception's argument by providing a variable in the except clause.

Raising Exceptions

You can raise exceptions in several ways by using the raise statement.

Syntax –

raise [Exception [, args [, traceback]]]

Here, *argument* is a value for the exception argument and *Exception* is the type
of exception. However, argument is optional; if not supplied, the exception
argument is None. For example, an exception can be a class, string or an object.
Most exceptions that Python core raises are classes, with an argument that is an
instance of the class.

In Python, you are allowed to create your own exceptions by deriving classes from
the standard built-in exceptions. (Python Exceptions Handeling)

Conclusion

This brings us to the end of this edition of the book. We can easily say that Python is a powerful language and that is the reason why all big companies are looking for programmers who have the knowledge of this dynamic language.

Before we end, let's summarize on what we have learned so far. The book began with basic introduction to Python, its features, how to install and set up. We also understood that Python has fewer syntactical constructs thus making it easy and readable. All Python fundamentals i.e. variables, data types, operators, lists, strings, loops, tuples and dictionary have been covered in the book.

We have also ensured that the concept of function, classes, and modules is covered for a better understanding of the language. The last section on exception handling can be useful in practical application.

To conclude, we can say that once you are clear on the basics of Python you will be able to create almost anything you want.

Thank you once again for downloading this book, hope it has given you a meaningful insightinto Python.

Works Cited

Python - Environment Setup. n.d. 2017.
    <https://www.tutorialspoint.com/python/python_environment.htm>.

Python Exceptions Handeling. n.d. 2017.
    <https://www.tutorialspoint.com/python/python_exceptions.htm>.

Book 2

Fortran Crash Course

By: PG WIZARD BOOKS

Step By Step Guide To Mastering Fortran Programming!

Fortran Crash Course: Step By Step Guide To Mastering Fortran
Programming!

© Copyright 2016 FLL Books- All rights reserved.

Fortran Crash Course: Step By Step Guide To Mastering Fortran
Programming!

Table of Contents

Introduction

Chapter 1: Learning The Basics of Fortran..55

Chapter 2: Working on Loops in Fortran...60

Chapter 3: Working With Strings and Arrays....................................53

Chapter 4: Manipulating the Variable Amounts...............................68

Chapter 5: Working With Conditional Statements............................72

Conclusion..75

Fortran Crash Course: Step By Step Guide To Mastering Fortran
Programming!

Introduction

Many beginners to coding worry that they are not going to be able to learn how to work with a new coding language. They feel that it is going to be too difficult to learn the language and that they will either not be able to do some of the programming that they want or that they just won't understand what is being said in the information. But when it comes to working with Fortran, you will find that learning how to code is a simple process.

In this guidebook, we are going to start out by talking about some of the information that comes with Fortran. We will also work on the first code for this language and discuss all the different parts that are going to be found inside of your code. This is a simple introduction to help you get some practice with writing your own code and ensures that you are able to get into some of the more complex situations that we will discuss later on.

Once we have these basics down, we are going to move on to some of the other things that you are able to do when it comes to working on your code in Fortran. We will take a look at writing some of your own loop statements, what strings and arrays are, working with conditional statements, and so much more. Even as a beginner, you will be able to use these options in order to make a really strong code and program as you want it.

When you are ready to get into coding and want to make sure that you are designing something that is strong and will work the way that you want, Fortran is one of the best coding languages to help you learn how to get it done. Make sure to use this guidebook to help you to get the basics to work with Fortran for all your coding needs.

Chapter 1: Learning the Basics of Fortran

As a beginner, you may have times that you are worried that a new coding language will be too hard for you to learn. You want to make your own programs, learn how to work in different operating systems, or have another goal that you would like to accomplish, but you worry that it is going to be too much work for you to accomplish because it will be too hard to do. But when it comes to learning how to work with Fortran (which is basically a contraction of Formula Translation), you are working with a great language that is designed for beginners, even for those that have no experience in coding before.

Fortran is considered one of the oldest programming languages that you can use and this can be a benefit as well as an issue. It is beneficial because you will be able to find this language anywhere that you want to look and the compiler, as well as the other add-ons, are all going to be free. It is a coding language that many scientists and engineers like to use because of all the functions that are built in and the fact that it is easily used with mathematical constructs. There are also many other things that you are able to do with this coding language, and since it is one of the oldest options around, you are sure to find lots of help and answers to ensure that you get the project done right.

What will I need to get started?

When you are ready to get started with Fortran, you will need to bring out a new text editor. There are several of these that are available, and you can choose the one that works for you. You need this because it allows you to out the codes so that the compiler, which you will need next, will be able to read out what you are doing and tell the computer how to behave. You are not able to use a word processor for this because these kinds of applications are not going to save files in plain text, which is required to make the compiler do its job.

Next on the list is the compiler. There are many options out there and most of them are going to be free as well so you can download these and not have to worry about adding in costs. Basically the compiler is going to take the words that you have written in the text editor and then change them around into something that the computer is actually able to read. You will just need to save your code and then the compiler will be able to execute it.

Some people find that working with an Integrated Development Environment, or IDE, is a great way to help make this a lot easier. This IDE is going to work similar to the text editor and the compiler in one so it saves you some time, especially when it comes to troubleshooting the written code. For those who are working on Windows computers, the IDE is really a good idea because it has an interface that is easy to sue and similar to what you are used to seeing on the Windows computer.

As mentioned, you could just use the text editor and the compiler, but the IDE does make it a bit easier to write your code. These combine both of the other two products in one and it is able to understand syntaxes of the code easily. In fact, it is going to be able to catch some of the errors that come up in the code as you are typing, saving a lot of time and accidents in the process.

The benefits of using Fortran for your coding

There are so many reasons why you may want to consider using Fortran as your coding language of choice. Whether you are looking to use it on the side as another coding language to master or this is one of the first coding languages that you are going to work with, the benefits of choosing this one are amazing. Some of the reasons that you would want to work with the Fortran coding language include:

- Easy to use: Fortran was designed for the beginner to learn how to use it. It is a simple language to work with and after looking at some of the codes in this book, you are sure to see that it is easy enough to learn how to work with.
- Has been around for a long time: Fortran is one of the first coding languages that came available for coders to use in their homes. This is a good thing because it is simplistic and easy to use. We are going to work on a few different codes inside of this guidebook and you will find that most of them are pretty straight forward and easy to write, even if you are a beginner. While some people feel that the fact that Fortran has been around for so long is a bad thing, it can mean so many good things for helping you to get the very best when working in coding.

- Great for the scientific community: this is a language that anyone is able to use for their own needs, but it is specifically important when it comes to the scientific community. If you have an occupation that is in this field, you will find that it is a good idea to learn how to use the Fortran code.
- Lots of programs still use it: even though this is an older coding language that you can use, there are still a lot of programs that use it. This means that you will have plenty of chances to use this programming language and to get some more practice.
- Can be modified for other languages: Fortran is one of the earliest coding languages that is out there so it has had many adaptations over the years. This means that there are versions that you are able to use and combine with some of your other programming languages. This makes it easier to do some of the more powerful things that you want to do with your coding.
- It is free: all the stuff that you need for Fortran, from the software itself to the IDE that you want to use with it, is all free to use. This makes it easier for everyone to use this language because you won't have to worry about all the costs that are associated with it.
- Has a big community: when it comes to using a brand new language, you want to make sure that you have a community that is able to answer your questions and make sure that you going on the right track. Since Fortran has been around for so long, there are many people who know how to use this and can be there to help you out.

There are many benefits to using the Fortran coding language. While some people prefer to go with another option that is easier or newer to use, there are still many people who want to work with Fortran because it is one of the first. It is a simplistic language to learn how to use even as a beginner, and it is able to get a lot of the coding and programming done that you would like. If you are looking for a coding language that is pretty easy to work with and is meant for beginners, you won't go wrong when choosing Fortran.

How to test my first code

Fortran Crash Course: Step By Step Guide To Mastering Fortran
Programming!

Now that we have spent some time talking about the things that you need to get started with the Fortran coding, it is time to test out one of our first codes. Once you have taken the time to install the IDE that you would like to use, it is time to double click on the icon so that the programming environment is going to open up. You can then create a brand new file but keep in mind that you may need to select on a Fortran file when you do this, just in case the IDE that you picked is able to read more than one language. So you will need to give it the extension of .f95 rather than of .txt so that you are able to compile these statements a bit later on.

One thing to keep in mind is that there are some other extensions that you are able to use when it comes to Fortran including .FOR, .F, and FPP. These extensions are going to tell the compiler was standards you are following with the work you do so make sure that you pick the one that you want and stick with it. You can experiment a bit to figure out which one you want to use.

So once you are done picking out the extension that you would like to use (we are going to stick with the .f95 one for now), we are going to need to type out the following code to get started:

```
program mytest

!this is a test

Print *, 'This is an output test'

end program mytest
```

After we have taken the time to type out this bit of code, it is time to execute it inside of the IDE. Your compiler will then go through and double check the parts of the code, looking to see if you have made any errors in the code before trying to run it. If there are any errors that show up, the IDE will let you know and ask you to fix it. If there aren't any troubles with the code, the compiler is going to generate and then execute the file. Basically, with this one you are going to find that the words "This is an output test" will show up on the screen if you typed it in the right way.

Breaking down this code

Fortran Crash Course: Step By Step Guide To Mastering Fortran
Programming!

Now that we have taken some time to write our own code, it is time to break it down to make a bit more sense. Like a lot of the other coding languages that are out there, the Fortran language is going to take care of the different lines of the code, which are called statements, and then decide what it is going to do with each of them. So in the first line, the program is going to state the name of the program that you are trying to work with.

Then moving on to the second line, you are working with a comment. This basically means that you are writing a little note for yourself or for the other programmers that are taking a look at the code. The compiler knows that it shouldn't execute the comment since this is just a little note. You can add in as many comments as you would like inside of the code to describe what the different parts are going to do.

The third line of the code is the output command that is going to tell the compiler what it is supposed to display on the screen. It is going to show up in a single quote. You can make this statement as long or short as you would like, just make sure that you are using the right options with it. And then in the last line, the statement is terminating, or ending, the program that you just write.

Now, this is a pretty basic option that we are working on and only has four lines. There are many options that you are able to do with Fortran that will use more lines to get it done depending on the things that you are doing inside the code. There are also a few versions of Fortran that will have the code look a bit different. Basically all of them need to have the four same parts including the program name, the output statements (you may have more than one of these in some cases), end of program, and comments if you need them.

Making sure that you have all the right parts in place in order to write the code is important to helping the compiler to work with you on creating the code. And while there are many different data types that you are able to use, as we will discuss as we go on in this guidebook, they can be as simple or as difficult as you need to make the code work.

Chapter 2: Working on Loops in Fortran

When you are working on writing your own code inside of Fortran, you need to understand how to work with loops. There are many different times when you will want the code to keep repeating something, or do a specific action more than once. With the most basic form of your code, you would need to write this part of the code over and over again. Now, if you just want the code to repeat a few times, this may not seem like such a big deal, but what happens when you want to write out the code 100 times? Rewriting the same part 100 times can get tiring and old pretty quickly.

But with loops, you are able to tell the compiler to repeat the same steps until the conditions are no longer true. This could be five times and it could be 1000 times, but you would just need to write out a few lines of code to make this happen. Rather than having to write out the same instructions over and over again, you are able to set up the loop to do the same functions over and over again.

There are several different components that are going to be found inside of a loop to make sure that it is going to work. The main components include:

- Step: this component is going to tell the compiler that the procedure will need to be repeated at least once.
- Start: this is going to tell the compiler that it is at the beginning of your loop.
- Stop: this is going to tell the compiler that it is at the end of your loop.
- Var: this is a variable. It is in charge of telling the compiler how many times that you would need to have your code repeated.

How do these loops work?

Loops are going to begin when you set the start and then you define the var. they will explore what concept you are working with inside the var and decide when the conditions have no longer been met so this will all start. As soon as your statement is executed once, the amount to the var is going

60

to go up by one so that you don't end up in an endless loop. So, if you want
to make a table that goes from one to ten, the var would start at one and
then each time it goes up by one until it reaches ten. Let's take a look at a
sample code that shows how the loop function is going to work:

```fortran
program loop_factorial

implicit none


        !definition of variables

        Integer::xfact=1

        Integer::x


        !computations of factorials

        Do x=1, 15

                Xfact=xfact*1

                Write*, x, xfact

        End do

End program loop_factorial
```

This one is a bit longer than what we are used to with the other code we
wrote, but it does show how the loop is going to work for you. This one is
going to make sure that the variable will keep going up by one each time
that you work with it, helping to keep things organized and to ensure that
you don't end up in an endless loop. If you do end up with a loop that
doesn't have a stop point, you are going to get stuck inside of the code and
have trouble getting out without closing the whole program.

There are a few different types of loops that you are able to work with.
Some are going to check the conditions of the statement before
determining whether or not to run the loop. If the conditions are not true
from the beginning, you are not going to get the loop to run at all and it is
going to head on to the next part of the code. This is known as the for loop.
And then the do while loop is going to run the loop at least one time, and
then run check the options to see if it meets the condition. The choice can

be the same, but it does depend on whether you want the code to run one
time or it doesn't matter.

The loop is one of the best things that you can work with when trying to
make your code look nice and organized when on Fortran. You will be able
to tell the loop how many times you would like it to run through the
program, just using a few lines rather than rewriting the code all of the
time. This is an efficient way to work inside of your code and ensures that
the code is still able to work properly.

Chapter 3: Working with Strings and Arrays

When you are working with Fortran, you will find that strings and arrays are great ways to help keep the code organized. There are certain ways that you will be able to work with these in order to get them to execute inside of the code properly. In this chapter, we are going to spend some time talking about what strings and arrays are and how you would be able to work with them inside your code.

What are strings?

Inside of the Fortran code, all characters are going to be seen as one of two elements. They are seen as either single characters or contiguous strings. So what is the difference between them? With a contiguous string, you will notice that their length for syntax declaration is going to be passed, they will allow you to do notations on the substring, they won't allow you to do notation on arrays, they can contain descriptors if needed, and in some cases there are going to be hidden arguments inside.

When you want to declare a string inside of Fortran, you are going to use rules that are similar to declaring some of the other variables. So in order to do this, you would use the following option (we are giving the string an assignment of 10):

specifier :: variable_name

character(len=10)::name

Now in addition to working on the string, you will be able to work on substrings, which are basically just smaller parts of the string. They are going to be any part of the program that is executed and you are able to extract them if you wish. For example, if you have a long string that is several sentences long, you could work on a substring and just take out a few of the words to make it easier to read if you want. Here is an example of how you would be able to take out substrings from the string inside the code:

```
program string_concatenation

implicit non


        character (len=5) :: name

        character (len=50) :: announcement

        character (len=50) :: message


        name = 'Dana Caulfield'

        announcement = 'This is'

        message = 'I would like to give you a warm welcome to Prescott
Academy!'


print *, announcement, name

print * , message

end program string_concatenation
```

With this option you are going to get the message "This is Dana Caulfield. I
would like to give you a warm welcome to Prescott Academy!" You are able
to choose how much of the message you would like to do and you can keep
it all on one line or on more than one. For example, you could choose to
just have "This is Dana Caulfield" show up on the screen if you would like.
This gives you some options to have a longer phrase there if you would like
while also keeping it so that you get smaller patches as well.

Concatenation

Another thing that we are going to take a look at when working inside of
Fortran is known as concatenation. You are going to notice that it will use
the (//) symbol in order to show that this is inside the code. The
concatenation property is the one that describes which programs are able

to link back to each other. Because of these connections that are established, the main goal is to either draw attention over to another branch in the program, or to make sure that the framework is solid. In some cases the links are going to be for two separate programs, but often the subjects are going to be single elements.

You can also work with a process that is known as trimming. This is when you want to cut out parts of the line that are not necessary so that you get the right result to show up. Since there can often be elements inside the program that aren't needed and are known as trailing blanks, the process of trimming is going to help to get rid of some of this clutter so that you are able to just use the portions that are needed. It also helps your compiler to be able to read through the code faster.

There are a lot of things that you are able to do with the strings inside of your projects and you will be able to mess around with them a bit to get the strings to work out the way that you want. But using concatenation and trimming will help to ensure that you are using the strings in the proper manner.

Arrays

Arrays are another important part of working on your code. They are going to be in charge of storing information, such as variables and characters, that are similar. If the piles of data aren't stored in the proper way, it is going to be really hard for the computer to be able to interpret them. However, when you use the arrays properly to put this information in the right places, the compiler is going to have a better chance at running the program and the functions will be executed in the proper way. Some of the things that you should remember about arrays to make it easier include:

- If you would like to specify the individual elements, you are going to need to address them using the subscripts. The first element is going to have the subscript of 1.
- If you see the term "extent' it is going to describe the elements that are along a dimension. Keep in mind that this is a numerical value.
- On the other hand, if you see the term rank, it is going to describe the dimensions that they have, using a numerical value as well.
- When you see the term "size" this is going to describe the elements that the array has, using numerical values again.
- The shape of the array is going to consist of elements.

- They are going to be declared with the attribute of dimension.
- They are going to be linked to memory locations that are contiguous.

There are two types of arrays that you are able to find inside of the Fortran language. The one-dimensional arrays are the ones that will serve as vectors while the two-dimensional arrays are the ones that will serve as the matrices.

Now that we know a little bit more about arrays, it is time to understand how you are going to be able to declare the arrays. Luckily this is a process that is pretty easy to complete. The rule is to specify the dimension that you desire, and then the compiler will be able to take a look at the elements that are involved and determine if they are an integer or real. For example, if you want to declare an array that is the Caulfield Lair and you want to give it seven elements, you would use the following code to make it happen:

real, dimension (7) :: Caulfield Lair.

Now you can also choose to declare an array that is two dimensional. Let's say that we are still using the example of Caulfield Lair from above, but we are going to make it so that the elements are 7 by 7. To do this, we are going to use the following syntax:

integer, dimension (7, 7) :: Caulfield Lair.

If you would like to make sure that you are assigning the right values to your arrays, you will find that the process is pretty simple. You just need to work on the array and then enter in the amount that you would like to use. You do have some choices when it comes to doing this because you can either do it on a single element that you want to change or you can work it out on the whole array. Let's take a look at an example of how this would work. Let's say that we want to add in the value of 3 to all of the elements would need the following code:

do I = 1, 7

Fortran Crash Course: Step By Step Guide To Mastering Fortran
Programming!

Caulfield Lair = i*3.0

end program do.

But on the other hand, if you would like to assign the value of 3 to just the first level of the array and then add different numbers to the other levels, you would need to use the following code to make it happen:

Caulfield Lair (1) = 3

Working with strings and arrays are a good way to make sure that you are getting the code to work in the right way. The strings are going to be statements that happen inside the code and make it easier for you to write out the different things that you would like to have happen, either by adding in the whole string to the code or just having a few parts as you see fit. The arrays are going to be responsible for holding large pieces of data in a way that is easier to look through and reach inside the code. Both of these are going to be important to ensuring that you get more out of the code and that it works the way that you want.

Chapter 4: Manipulating the Variable Amounts

Now at this point we are going to take some time to look at the different
operators and variables that you are able to use inside of your code. So far
at this point we have learned a bit about how to create a simple program.
But there is a lot of manipulation that you are can do inside the code and
operators are a great way to help you to do this. The operators inside of
Fortran is going to be a great way to do mathematical functions while also
getting these results to show up on the screen. With all that we have
learned so far about this program, it is now possible to work on a short
program on our own that will help to manipulate the amounts of variables.
So basically inside of this chapter, we are going to learn how to make our
program in Fortran do some basic math.

First we need to take a look at what the variable is all about. A variable is
basically a little container that is going to store information inside of the
memory of the computer. You are able to use these to hold either one or
more value of your choice, and you are able to assign this either at the
beginning of your block of code or when the code is being executed.

Assigning a variable is going to be pretty easy to accomplish. You will just
need to use the (=) in order to pick the value that you would like to use
along with the variable. You are able to add more than one value to the
same variable if you would like to store them together in the code, but for
the most part, it is just going to be one variable that you are working with.
You can add in many different variables inside of the code, but the
operators that we are going to talk about in a minute help to make it easier
to get this all done.

Before we get too far into making this kind of program, we are going to take
some time to work with operators. While these are pretty simple, there are
some times when they can seem confusing and will make you wonder what
they mean. The trick with these is to not think of them as mathematical
symbols. For example, when it comes to writing out a = 2, you should see
this as the value of 2 is going to be stored inside the memory of your
computer that is labeled as a. Here is another example that you can use:

a = 2

b = 3

c = a + b

In the statement that we did above, you will see that the value of 2 is going to be stored as the memory location that is a and then you will see that the value of 3 is stored in the memory location that is called be. And then when you add the values of a and b together, you are going to store that result under the memory location of c. Keep in mind with this one that you are not able to write out this kind of equation as a + b = c because the compiler is going to see this as an error. The one variable needs to be on the left-hand side of your symbol and then you can have as many of the variables as you would like on the right-hand side, but mixing these around are going to cause an error message.

Arithmetic operators

Now that we have looked at some examples of operators, it is time to work with some of the operators that you need. Not all of the math symbols that you will need are going to show up on the keyboard, but the Fortran does have some of its own symbols that you are able to use in order to represent the different math operands that you are able to use. Some of the most common arithmetic operators that you are able to use on your language includes:

- (+): this is the one that you are going to use for addition
- (-): this is the one that you are going to use for subtraction in the code.
- (*): this is the one that you are going to use for multiplication
- (/): this is the one that you can use for division

One thing to note with these is that you can use more than one of the symbols, whether you are using three addition signs or an addition and a division symbol, inside the same part of code. You are able to use as many of these as you want, but you need to use the order of operands to do it. This means that you will need to do all of the multiplication, then the division, addition, and subtraction, going from left to right to make sure that the compiler is going to give you the right answer.

Other parts of your code

As a beginner, you will wonder what all the blanks, or the skip positions, are inside of the program. Some people choose to write out their programs without using these at all, but for the most part, the programmers like to include these inside of their code in order to make it easier to read. You are able to choose how you would like to use a skip position, but you should include at least a few to make sure that your code is easier to read through.

There are also some special characters that you are able to work with inside of your code. These are used in order to deliver the function that you want. These are going to seem pretty simple and plain but you need to be careful about how you use them. If you use them the wrong way or place two of them into the code right next to each other, you could end up with conditions that cancel each other. Some of the special characters that are found inside of Fortran and that you should watch out for include:

- (/): this one is going to specify another line
- ("): to output strings
- (:): this is going to terminate a list
- () this is going to categorize the descriptors.

Descriptors can be a tool that you are able to use and they are variables that are going to specify the amount of data that is required for a conversion. It is a good idea to keep track of the usage of these since the process may not end unless you add in the right descriptor is placed inside. Some of the descriptors that you can use include:

- A: repetition
- D: this one is for digits next to your decimal points.
- E: this is for an exponential number
- M: this is the minimum amount of digits.
- W: this is width in total characters.

Fortran Crash Course: Step By Step Guide To Mastering Fortran
Programming!

You are going to be able to use all of these different parts to help you to get the code to work the way that you would like. You can mix and match a few of the parts to get the variable to be the right number, to store it in the right place inside the code and to do so much more. When you are able to add in the operators of the Fortran code, work with the blanks or the skip positions to make the code easier to use, and add in the special characters and the descriptors to the code, you are going to get a lot of power and options inside of the code.

Chapter 5: Working with Conditional Statements

At this point, we are going to take some time to look at the if statements. These are the most basic of the conditional statements and you will find that they are pretty straightforward. With this one, you will set the condition that needs to be met as well as the action that will show up at the same time with it. If the user puts in an input that matches, you will see that the program puts up the action that you choose. On the other hand, since this is a simple equation to work with, when the user puts in an input that is seen as false, the program is just going to end because you didn't set up an action.

So for this one, let's say that you just want people who are 18 to be able to get into the website. You would set up the if statement to accept any answer that is 18 and above. If the user places their age inside to be 20, the action (such a statement that you choose) will be executed by the compiler. But if the user puts in that their age is 16, then the program is going to see that this answer is false compared to the conditions that you set, and since you are using the if statement, nothing is going to happen.

Now there are some issues that can come up with this, but let's just focus on learning the syntax and getting this part down. Take a look at the syntax below for this:

if (x == 1) then

print *, 'turn left'

end if

The logical operator is the one that is used in this example along with the statement of if..then..end if. Note the expression that comes after the if statement. It is going to provide you with a test, something that is necessary when you are trying to imply a condition. In this case, we are going to assume that the "x" variable is an integer. One of the values that it can be is equal to 1. Interpreting this as a logical operation, the program is going to test to see if the value of the variable is 1. Then it will check if this is true or not. If your variable is 1, then the statements that come next will

72

be executed which in this case would be the words "turn left". Then the end
if is going to terminate the program that you are working on.

The if...else statements

As we mentioned in the last part, the if statement is going to be pretty basic
and there are some issues with it. Your user may very well be 16 years old
and it isn't a good idea to have the program just end if they put in this
answer. You most likely will want to have some message come up at least,
so that the user doesn't assume that something is wrong with the program.
For example, if they put that their age is over 18, you would want to set it
up to say something like "Welcome to the site!" and then have the next
action be that they can get in. But if they put in that they are 16 or
something else, you would rather have a message like "Only those over 18
are allowed in the game!" than having the program just end.

The if...else statement is able to help you to do that. You would set it up like
the first part that we had above, but then you would add the else that
catches anything that is considered false by the compiler based on the
conditions that you set. This allows you to have an answer, any answer,
come up regardless of what input the user is giving to you. This makes it
much more clean cut and easier to deal with and doesn't leave the user
wondering what is wrong with the user.

In addition, you are able to make it so that there are several options that
come up. Let's say that you would like to have someone pick out their
favorite color of either red, green, yellow, or blue. You would just need to
write out more of the else sections of this code would just keep going.
Another really useful thing for you to learn how to use inside of your
Fortran code is the conditional statement. These are really great because
they allow you to have some extra power and choices inside of the code.
These will allow you to put in the conditions that need to be met in order to
get different statements or actions to occur. They can be really simple, such
as the if statement, where you will only have an action happen when the
answer is inputted is true compared to your conditions, you can have it so
that a different action will happen based on if the answer is true or false
based on your condition, or you can give the user some choices.

You can decide what conditions need to be met before you allow the user to
put in their information. This allows the code to keep things simple and it
can look at your conditions before executing what you would like to have
happen. You can make these as complex or as simple as you would like, but
remember that you do need to base these on Boolean expressions. You

have to leave the answer as either true or false based on the conditions that you set.

Don't worry if this sounds complicated right now. We are going to take some time to look over the different conditional statements that you are able to work with and help you to get the results that you want, no matter what kind of conditional statement you are working with.

The if statements

down the line, taking a look through each condition and statement that you put onto the screen. You can also add in a catch or break at the end so if the user picks pink or another color that isn't listed there so they still get an answer.

There are so many options that you are able to do with the if...else statements and they can really open up a lot of what you are able to do inside of your code. You can make them as simple or as complex as you would like, adding in more sections or just having a true and false option. Mess around with this a bit and see what you are able to come up with on your if...else statements.

Conclusion

Working in a coding language can be difficult no matter who you are. Many beginners are worried that they are not going to be able to find the answers to getting started or that it is just going to be too hard for them to pick out how to work with this code. But when it comes to working in Fortran, you will find that writing out a code can be nice and simple and it won't take that long for you to learn it and start working on your own.

This guidebook is going to take some time to help you learn how to work with the Fortran code. We are going to start out with writing some of our own codes while learning about some of the basics that come with Fortran. We will then move on to working with strings and arrays, understanding how the loops work, and even working with conditional statements. These are actually really important parts of working with a coding language, but since Fortran is so simple to work with that you will be able to add them into a code in no time.

When you are ready to get started on writing some of your own codes and want to get into the world of coding, working with Fortran is one of the best options to help you to get this all done. It is an older language that is meant for beginners and you will be able to catch on to it in no time at all. Use this guidebook to learn what you need to know in order to get the Fortran language to work for you.

Book 3

Android Crash Course

By: PG WIZARD BOOKS

Step by Step Guide To Mastering Android Programming!

Android Crash Course: Step by Step Guide To Mastering Android Programming!

Android Crash Course: Step by Step Guide To Mastering Android
Programming!

Table Of Contents

Introduction

Chapter 1: An Overview of Android..80

Chapter 2: The Architecture of the Android Operating System..........85

Chapter 3: Working on Your First Project..89

Chapter 4: Running the App..92

Chapter 5: Doing Updates with the SDK Manager...........................95

Chapter 6: How to Publish an Android App.....................................98

Conclusion..100

Introduction

Working with the Android operating system can be a great experience. Unlike some of the other coding languages and operating systems out there, Android is the language that you will work with for mobile devices rather than for your computer. With that being said, you are still able to work on the computer, using an emulator, so that you can check out if the app that you create is going to work properly or not.

If you are interested in creating some of your own apps with the help of the Android operating system, this is the guidebook that is going to help you to get it done. It is a simple program to learn how to use, and this guidebook is going to make it easier than ever to get started. We will talk about some of the basics of working with the Android operating system as well as how it is all set up for you to use. Once that is done, we are going to learn how to download the Android operating system, set up the emulator, write your first code, and even make some changes to it later on. There is so much that you are able to do with the help of this operating system and we are going to take a look at some of the best parts of it with this guidebook.

When you are ready to learn a new coding language for your mobile devices, and you want to be able to create some of your own applications, make sure to check out this guidebook for the basics on how to get started from doing updates, to installing the software and even creating some of your first programs.

Chapter 1: An Overview of Android

If you are someone who likes to work in programming and even on smartphones, then the Android operating system is a great option for you to use. Android is an operating system that is based off Linux, which makes it really easy for you to use. The user interface is considered as direct manipulation based and it is one that will be used and designed to work with tablets and smartphones that are touchscreens as well as cars, televisions, and wristwatches that are compatible with this technology. With the operating system, you are able to make use of the touch inputs which will be able to correspond with actions that are done in the real world, such as pinching, swiping, and tapping.

With all of the things that Android is able to work with, you are going to find many different projects that you are able to create. Android is a really low-cost operating system that is ready made and can be customized to the needs that you have. And since it is able to be used with other high-tech devices, it has become really popular with a wide range of technology companies. Add in that this is an open source operating system (which means that programmers are able to use it and make changes as they see fit), it is easy to use on your own projects, and you can even find a large community of developers who can help you out.

There are many features that you are going to find with the Android system. You will be able to use it with other languages to work on your device, it has the power that you need to compete with the Apple operating system and Windows 8.1 it is able to store all the information that you need, works with your Wi-Fi, and even has an interface that is intuitive for the user. These are some of the features that you can enjoy while using the Android operating system and with the new innovations that are always coming out thanks to this code being open sourced, you are sure to find other benefits that will help you to get your projects done.

Android is one of the best-operating systems out there for devices like tablets, televisions, and mobile phones. There are billions of these devices hooked up to the Android system, and it has quickly become one of the largest mobile platform bases with a huge growth potential in the future. In fact, according to the Google Corporation, it is believed that more than a million new devices are activated with Android each day.

Android Crash Course: Step by Step Guide To Mastering Android Programming!

The interface

By default, the user interface in Android is going to be base don the touch inputs of the user with options like pinching, swiping, and tapping on the objects, or the keyboard on the screen of the device. So basically this is an operating system that is designed to respond to the input of the user right away, and it includes a smooth touch interface to make things easier. You will also find that this operating system is going to put to use the vibration feature of the device, so the user is able to get some haptic feedback.

The internal hardware that comes with this operating system, such as accelerometers, gyroscopes, and proximity sensors are used by the applications, and you can use it for adjusting the orientation of the screen, using remote controls, and even change up the home screen for the different pages that you use. Basically, this is a very intuitive interface that the user is going to love because it responds to their touches and it has so many different options that they are able to use.

Managing the memory

For the most part, the devices that run on Android are going to use battery. So if you want to make sure that the battery life is going to last longer, you will want to have a RAM that will consume less power because they will not get a continuous source of power like some of your desktop devices. Whenever the app is minimized, or it isn't in use, it is going to be placed inside the memory automatically. Yes, these applications are going to be open still, but this method is going to help to prevent it from consuming all the resources of the system; they will simply wait in the background until you decide to call them back up.

This is great for the Android device because you will be able to call it back up as needed, but it helps to save the limited RAM that you have. The RAM is limited because you want to make sure that it doesn't waste out all the battery power that you have this device. Luckily, this system is going to be good at managing some of your applications. If it notices that your memory is running low, it is simply going to terminate the processes that aren't being used, closing up the oldest applications first to save room.

Android Crash Course: Step by Step Guide To Mastering Android
Programming!

Security and privacy

Many people are worried about getting on a new operating system is whether it is
going to keep your privacy safe and if it is secure enough to work on the apps
with. There are many operating systems that promise to be amazing when it
comes to your security and privacy, but some of them may fall short at some
times and won't provide the benefits that you are looking for. But when it comes
to the Android operating system, you are going to get all the benefits of a lot of
security and privacy, simply by the way that the system is set up to deal with the
work that you are doing and since you get to determine how all the apps interact
on the computer and get to give each of them permission before they get any
information, you know that your privacy is always going to be safe.

The applications that you use in Android are going to run inside the sandbox,
which is basically an area of your system that is isolated and will not have access
to the other resources unless you give permission for this when you install the
application. Before you install a new application, you will also need to give
permission in order to get it on the system. This is going to take a bit more time
through the installation process, but it helps to prevent bugs in the applications,
limits documentation, and helps to keep your information secure and private no
matter what.

Works with different languages

One of the nice things about working with the Android operating system is that it
is able to work with many other coding languages. Almost all of the major coding
languages are supported on these devices, and the list is currently at over 100
languages. This makes it easy for the Android device to adapt to what you want to
use. It also supports Java so that if you want to create something to work online,
the Java language is going to be easy to use.

These are just some of the things that you are going to fall in love with when you
get started on the Android platform. It is great to work with mobile devices, no
matter what kind you have, it has a lot of speed and stability so that you know
that your coding will work out well, and you can develop many different kinds of
applications, in many different coding languages if you want, without too much
hassle.

The benefits of working with the Android operating system

Android Crash Course: Step by Step Guide To Mastering Android
Programming!

When it comes to working with an operating system that works out well with your mobile devices, none of them are going to be as great as the Android operating system. There are other options, but the Android operating system is going to work on billions of devices all over the world. Some of the benefits that you will be able to enjoy with this operating system include:

- Easy to use: working with the Android operating system can be really easy. You are going to learn how to create some of your own apps in no time, and then you can bring out your own creativity to work with Android or to create the apps that you dream about.
- Works well with mobile devices: the whole idea of using the Android operating system is so that you are able to use it to create apps that are good for your mobile devices. This can include things like televisions, tablets, and smartphones. You can use the emulator that is available for your computer, or your own device, in order to create an app and then have a chance to try it out to see if it works.
- Works with the Java language: you will need to know how to work with the Java language if you want to work on an Android app. This is a basic website and online building language that is easy to use, but it is important that you learn how to use this ahead of time.
- Allows you to create and sell your own apps: one of the reasons that a lot of people will choose to go with the Android operating system is because they have some ideas for apps that they want to use and hope to sell. There are millions of people who use the Android operating system on their devices, and they are always looking for new apps and games to work with. Some people choose to sell the apps for free, and others will make money off of the added space they sell or the cost of the app. This is a great way to make some extra money if you like to work with apps.
- The user interface is easy to work with: this user interface is meant to be really interactive. In fact, it is going to work mainly by the user working with their hands and fingers rather than relying on buttons and clicks like the other operating systems that you may be used to. This can make it easier for you to learn how to make apps that the customer will love because they can work on it in real time without all the extras going on around it causing it to be slower.
- A big community to ask questions with: the Android system has a big community of people you are able to meet with, ask questions of, and so much more when you need help. Android has been around for a long time,

and it has a lot of devices that will use this system to get things done. This makes it easier for you to use the operating system and to get it to work the way that you would like.

There are many options that you can choose when it comes to making a mobile operating system work for your app. Some people will use the Windows system and other times you will want to go with the Apple iOS. But none have the wide range and all the flexibility that you need from the Android operating system, and this is why so many people choose to go with it. With billions of devices that use this operating system and a million more being added each day, it is no wonder that people love being able to use and learn how to use Android.

Chapter 2: The Architecture of the Android Operating System

Before we get too far into developing our programs with the Android operating system, it is important to know some of the architecture that comes with this program and where things will work together. The framework of the application is easier to understand if we know how things are going to be arranged and will work inside of the operating systems. Since this is an operating system that is based on Linux, you will see that the two are very similar if you have worked with Linux in the past. For those who have never worked on Linux at all, you will notice that the layout of the language is pretty simple to use and you will catch on pretty quickly. Let's take a look at the architecture of this operating system.

Basic applications

The first applications that you are going to see are the basic ones. These are some of the options like the application to make calls, for your music player and camera and more. They don't have to come from Google, and sometimes Google isn't going to provide them at all, but you will be able to use the Google play store in order to develop these kinds of applications and make it so that they are available for everyone to use. You can also develop the apps with Java and then install them into the device that will integrate with the Android operating system.

Application framework

This is the part of the system that is going to be used for developing the applications. This framework is available with many different interfaces, and the developers will pick out which interface they want to use based on the standards that are important to them. By using these frameworks, you are going to save a lot of time and effort because it is not necessary to code out all of the tasks. There are also some different entities that come with the framework, and the options available are going to change based on the framework that you want to use.

Activity manager

When you are using the activity manager, you are using the part of the program that is responsible for managing the different activities that control the app life cycle. It is going to have many different states, and the activity manager will be able to handle all of these. The applications are going to consist of many different types of activities, and each of these activities is going to have its own life cycle. Whenever you launch up a new application, one main activity is going to be started. You will be able to pull up a window when needed in order to see every activity inside an app.

Resource managers

If you have some applications that are going to require some kind of external resources, such as an external string, these are going to be managed with the help of your resource manager. These parts are going to be able to allocate the resources in the way that is standard for your device and will make sure that everything works together well.

Libraries

There are several libraries that you are able to us in Android in order to make sure that you are using the right codes, to save time, and to make your work more powerful. All of the native libraries for Android are going to be found inside of this layer, but all of them are going to be written using either the C++ or the C language. The capabilities that are found inside these libraries are going to be similar to what you find in the application layer on the top of the Linux kernel. Some of the things that you are going to find inside of these libraries on Android will include:

- Surface manager: this is the compositing window in manager and display.
- System C libraries: these are the basic libraries of C that are going to be targeted for the ARM or embedded devices.
- A media framework: this could include options for playback, recording, video, audio, and more.

- OpenGL ES libraries: this is the one that is needed for the graphics on the device.
- SQLite: this is a database engine. This one, in particular, is a smaller version that works better on Android without using up as much memory space.

All of these are going to come together in order to help you to find out the codes that you would like to use inside your program. You can use these as a simple way to get started on the app that you would like to use or as some suggestions as to what you would need to do next. You can always add in some of the other parts that you would like if the code really needs it, but this is one of the best places to start as a beginner in order to get your basics down and to start writing some of your own code.

Android Runtime

You will find that the Dalvik Virtual Machine is the part that is in charge of the runtime for all Android devices. This is a virtual machine that is going to be used for your embedded devices as well as an interpreter for bytecode. They are going to have lower memories and can be a bit slower than you are used to since they run on batteries. You will find that the Java libraries are also going to be on these devices which means that you will be able to use them.

Kernel

When it comes to using the Android operating system, you will be using the Linux Kernel 2.6. This is going to include all the electronic equipment that you need, and many of the processes are going to be similar to what you will find with the Linux operating system to make things easier. Between the software and hardware of Android, you are going to see that the kernel will behave similar to the abstraction layer in the hardware and will include essential parts like the keypad, camera, and display. The kernel is also going to be in charge of handling things like the networking and device drivers.

Keep in mind that working with the Linux system means that everything is going to be in the form of a kernel. This helps to add in some security to the system and makes the whole program easier to use. If you have ever worked with the Linux system, you are used to how easy the Linux operating system is to do a lot of different tasks, and this is going to translate over to the work that you are doing over on the Android operating system as well.

Now that you know a bit more about the different parts that come with the Android operating system and how it does work quite well with the Linux system, it is time to move on to downloading this software properly and working on a few of your very first projects to make things easier.

Chapter 3: Working on Your First Project

Now that we have taken the time to learn more about the Android system, it is time to work on our first project. This one is going to be pretty simple to learn, but will help you to get a feel for how all of this works for some of the other topics we will bring up later on. But the first step that we need to take when getting started is to install the Android Studio.

To start with this, we need to see if the Java Development Kit, or the JDK, is installed on your computer or not. Some computers come with this already in place so that can save you time. For a PC, you need to click on Start, Run, type in the word "cmd" and then press enter to see if it is there. If you are on a Mac computer, you will use the Spotlight to search for the Terminal and then choose the top result. If this is on the computer, use the prompt "java-version." If a command is not found, you will need to visit the Oracle website and download the JDK on your computer.

Once this is done, it is time to go online and download the right version of the Android Studio for your computer. When this has had time to download the right way on the computer, you can click on Next to move on to the following screen. At this location, you will need to pick the setup that you want to use (standard is usually the best one) before clicking on Next and accepting the license agreements. At this point, the Android Studio is going to finish up the download, and you are ready.

For each version of Android that you are using, you will find that it contains a version of SDK for you to work with. The setup wizard is going to help you to get the updated versions of this. It is important to have the SDK because it helps you to set up the Android Virtual Device, the part that allows you to test your new apps on it and you can give it the right customizations for your own personal configuration.

So go back to the Welcome Screen of the Android Studio and click Configure. You should see a new menu that offers you a lot of options, and you will want to pick the one that says SDK Manager. A new window should appear when you click on this, and a series of folders, checkboxes, and statuses are going to show up. If you just downloaded the Android Studio, you should have the latest version of SDK

Tools as well as some of the other tools to make the program work. If you see that
an update is still available for this, the box will be ticked, and you can choose
whether or not you want to take this.

Once you have had time to get the latest version of the SDK Manager on your
computer (taking the time to update it if you need), it is time to create one of your
first programs inside of the Android operating system.

Creating the OMG Android

Now it is time to start working on your very first project, and we are going to start
out pretty simple, using the Hello, World! Kind of idea that the other coding
languages go with. The idea behind this one is to give you some options and
familiarity with using Android so that you can do some of the bigger projects later
on.

The nice thing that you will notice about the Android Studio is that it comes with
a nice tool that will give you the steps that you need to get this project started.
You will just need to get on the Welcome Screen, click that you want to start a
New Android Studio Project, and then the screen for project creation will show
up. You are allowed to place an application name, and we are going to call this
one OMG Android. For the company domain just put in your name. You may
notice that the Package Name is going to change at this time to make a reverse
domain name based on what you call the application and your company. This is
going to be like a unique identifier so that the app is easily found among all the
others.

Set the project location to the hard drive location that you would like before
clicking on Next. On this screen, you are going to tell the system which devices
and operating systems you would like to make the app work with. You probably
don't want to make an app that will work with each Android device, but you can
narrow this down to just smartphones or just tablets if you would like. For this
one, to keep things easier, we are going to target the Android phone (you should
see that this is the default option selected along with the Minimum SDK).

You can then click on Next to get to the following screen to choose what activity
will happen for the app. A good way to think about this is as a window inside the

Android Crash Course: Step by Step Guide To Mastering Android
Programming!

app that will be able to show what content will be interactive with the user. You can use this activity as a popup or as the while window. Inside of this template, the activities are going to range from being blank with an Action Bar all the way to one that has an embedded Map View. But for this project, we are going to keep things simple and work with Blank Activity before clicking Next.

At this point, you are almost to the coding. We are going to go through and use the default options with this and then click on the Finish button. There will be a few minutes for the Studio to go through and finish off the project and sometimes you will notice that it is going through all the different steps and putting out information about what it is doing. The nice thing is that with this IDE, a lot of work is going to be done for you.

After a few minutes, the Studio is going to finish building up this project. This project so far is going to be empty since we didn't put in any code to it, but it will contain all the information that is needed to be launched on one of the Android devices. At this point, you should see that there are three windows that are open on the Android Studio. On the left is going to be the project folder, the middle will have a preview of what this looks like on the Nexus 5, and then the last window is going to show the layout of the project.

Right now the project is pretty empty and will not show much up on the screen, but you will be able to make changes to that later on and add in some words as well as some other really cool things. But for now, you have created a good program so let's take that a step further in the next chapter and not only add in some of the words or phrases that you need to work with inside this operating system, but also learn how to make the app run with your emulator or with the Android   device.

Chapter 4: Running the App

So in the last chapter, we spent some time making a pretty basic app. We learned
how to get it all setup and that the Android Studio is really great at setting the
defaults that you want to use and which will ensure that you have it named the
right way and ready to go. But so far the app doesn't have any words in it for
others to see or any other actions, and it isn't running in a way that the other
Android apps will be able to use. This chapter is going to take some time to add in
these two options so that you can make your app start to work.

Running the app on an Emulator

So with the example that we did in the previous chapter, we took the time to
create our first app, but now we need to figure out how to run that. If you already
own an Android device, you are able to use this to run and test out the app, but if
you don't have a device, you can choose to work with an emulator. The Android
Studio is going to include the abilities that you need to set up a software-based
device right on your computer. This basically means that you can run apps, debut
the app, and look through a website on your computer, but it will work as if you
were on the Android app. You will be able to set up as many emulators on your
computer, and you can mess around with the screen size, version of the platform,
and more to really see how the app is going to work.

If you went through the setup wizard properly on the last steps, you could already
have the emulator in place on your computer. But we are going to take a moment
to set up a brand new emulator in case you missed this option before or if you
would like to choose a second emulator on the computer.

To get started on this is to click on the AVD Manager. You should be able to look
inside of the toolbar for the icon that has the Android popping up and is beside a
device with a purple display. The Android Studio is going to have one of these
setups that you are able to use, and you will be able to see some details about the
type of the emulator, the API that it uses, and the CPU instructions.

But if you would like to create a brand new AVD, you will just need to click on the
Create Virtual Device. Now you will need to come up with some choices. For the
first one, you will need to decide which device you would like to emulate. You
should be able to look over to the left and see a list of categories that basically list
all of the devices that you will be able to emulate and then you can see the
different devices in each category. To make things simple, we are going to click on
the Phone category and choose the Nexus S. once you pick this one, click on the
Next.

Now you also need to decide on the Android version you would like to use. There
are a few options that are available, and we are going to pick one of them,
Lollipop. Check that when you are on this that the ABI column shows a value of
x86 to ensure that the emulator is going to run at a good speed. Click on the Next
button. This page should basically be a confirmation screen that you should
double check before clicking on Finish and ending this process.

At this point, you have created a brand new virtual device that will allow you to
test out your app. You should close down the AVD Manager and then head back
to your main screen of the Android Studio. For the final step, you will click on
Run before another window shows up and you can choose which device you want
to test this app on. You shouldn't have any of the devices running here so you can
start with the AVD that you created earlier, just make sure to click on the Launch
Emulator and that the AVD is selected before clicking on OK.

Here you will need to give the emulator some time to load up, and you may even
need to do this a few times to get it right. Once all of this is loaded properly, you
will be able to see what there is of the running app.

So now that this emulator is all set up, it is time to add a bit more to the code that
we did earlier so that we can see how it is going to work on other Android devices.
We are going to keep this one simple right now, but you can always expand on
this to get more out of it. So to start on this, you will need to go to
res/values/strings.xml and then double click on this file. We are going to change
this so that we can make it a bit more personal and have some fun with it. Here is
the syntax of what you should type in:

<string name = "hello_world">I am learning Android!

</string>

You would be able to change up the code to say anything that you would like inside of this part of the code, making the string a lot longer, changing up the message, and so much more. This is just a great little way of showing how the code can work. But with this one, you have created your first app and even made some changes to make it a bit more personalized. You will just need to click on Run when it is done, and the message that you wrote out should show up on the screen.

Chapter 5: Doing Updates with the SDK Manager

Now we are going to take some time to do a bit more with the app that you want
to create. This is all going to work regardless of the version of SDK that you would
download on your computer so even if one of the older versions is there; it will
still work. If you would like to make sure to open up the SDK Manager from
inside the project, you will just need to click on the button that has the downward
arrow with your Android peeking above it. When we are done with this section,
we are going to be able to make a lot of changes to the app, and we will have one
that has a PNG image, has an editable text field, and so much more.

So at this point, we need to have our "Hello, World!" app open and ready to go on
the device, or you can use the emulator if that is the method that you would like
to work with so that the message is showing. But now it is time to take this over to
the next level.

Getting started on this project

For this one, we are going to take a moment to look ahead. The first thing that
you will want to do with this step of the project is to make sure that the app is
going to be simple. You don't want to add in a lot of complexities at this part
because this can slow down the app, introduces some more bugs to the system,
and just makes it more difficult for the user to work with. You only want to add in
extra parts if you really need it for the app to work properly, but right now this is
going to take some more time and work than what we want to work with at the
time.

So to get started, we are going to need to open up the
app/res/layout/activity_main.xml. If you are able to see the .raw and .xml file,
you will be good to go. But if this is not showing up, you will need to go to the
bottom of your screen and see if you need to switch all of this over to the Text
mode. All we will do at this point is work to get rid of some of the attributes that
are just padding to it. The Studio often adds these things to the .xml file on its
own, but it can make it harder to work on the file. You are going to want to look
for and delete all of these lines before we continue:

android:paddingLeft="@dimen/activity_horizontal_margin

android:paddingRight=@dimen/activity_horizontal_margin

android:paddingTop=@dimen/activity_vertical_margin

android:paddingBottom=@dimen/activity_vertical_margin

If you went through all of this and did it the proper way, your new .xml file is going to look like the following:

<RelativeLayout

xmlns:android=http://schemas.android.com/apk/res/android

xmlns:tools=http://schemas.android.com/tools

android:layout_width="match_parent"

android:layout_height="match_parent"

tools:context=".MainActivity">

<TextView

android:text="@string/hello_world

android:layout_width="wrap_content"

android:layout_height="wrap_content"/>

</RelativeLayout>

At this point, we will need to look for the Mainactivity.java part of the code. You will need to look on the left pane that is inside of Studio and then double click on it. We are going to take a moment to look at the very first piece of code, and you will need to move out a few of the lines including the following:

@Override

public boolean onOptionsItemSelected(MenuItem item){

```
//Handle action bar item clicks here. The action bar will

//automatically handle clicks on the Home/Up button, so long

//as you specify a parent activity in AndroidManifest.xml.

int id = item.getItemId();


//noinspection SimplifiableIfStatement

if (id == R.id.action_settings){

return true;

}


return super.onOptionsItemSelected(item);

}
```

You should be careful when you are doing this to make sure that you are leaving the final curly brace in its place when you delete the other options. This is the curly brace that is going to close up your class ahead of it, and you want to make sure that it is still there. Now that all the housekeeping work has been done, it is time to get to work and give the Activity a new life of its own.

Chapter 6: How to Publish Your Android App

Now that we have had some time to create our own app a little bit and learn how to manage the app in a way that makes it have less stuff in the way and so that it does more of the work that you want, it is time to learn how to publish your own app. You are going to work with making a lot of different types of apps over the years when you get familiar with working with the Android operating system and it is likely that you will at some point want to be able to publish one of the apps to make some money or for other people to be able to use it as well. In this chapter, we are going to spend some time learning how to take one of the apps that you create and getting it published.

The first thing to know is that when creating an Android app, you will need to publish it on the Google Play store. This means that you will need to create your own account using the Google Play Developer Console. This account is going to cost a little bit of money to create, about $25 at the publishing of this book, but considering the other parts of the operating system are free, this isn't so bad. The reason that there are fees with this account is that the Google company wants to keep out people who would make duplicate or fake accounts and helps to avoid people flooding the store with bad apps that no one else wants.

After you have gone through and created the account and paid the beginning fees, you are going to have your own Google Play Developer Account. You will be able to choose as many apps as you would like to publish on this account and you can choose whether you would like to publish those apps for free for others to use or in a manner to make money through the system. Some people are turned away by the fees, but if you are looking to make some money with this system on your apps by selling them, you will find that you can quickly make this $25 back. You can also allow ads to be on your app and earn some ad-revenue if you would like.

So to get this started, you just need to visit the site https://developer.android.com/distribute/index.html. Then you will just need to follow the steps that come up on the prompts to help you figure out what you are supposed to do to finish the account. In the end, you will finish creating your own developer account, pay the fees that are associated with the account to get it started, and then complete the process.

Android Crash Course: Step by Step Guide To Mastering Android
Programming!

At this point, you are probably done with creating your append are ready to upload it into the system. You will just need to upload the app file in a manner that is similar to how you would attach a link or a document into your email. Then you will be asked to take a survey. This is not something that you will be able to skip out on because the system wants to know about the different factors and features about your app. Some of the questions that it is going to ask is about whether there are inappropriate contents inside and if there are any age restrictions on using the app.

After you are done with setting up your account and getting the app to upload inside of the program, you are going to need to give Google a few days in order to validate the app. You will be able to add in as many of these apps as you would like over time, but you still need to give it a few days before it is going to show up inside the app store.

And that is all that you would need to do in order to get the app to work inside of the Google Play Store. You will be able to choose to offer the game for free, add some ad revenue into the system to make money, or charge for people to use the app in the first place. There are many options about the type of apps that you are able to use, and since it is so easy to add it to the Google store, you will be able to develop the app, get it put up, and move on to the next project in no time.

Conclusion

The Android operating system is a great one for you to learn how to use whenever you are looking to create an app or another program that works on phones, tablets, televisions and other mobile options. It is based on the Linux system which makes it easy to learn how to use (especially if you already know how to use this system), and you will find that over 100 coding languages are recognized on Android, so you are able to pick the one that is best for you.

In this guidebook, we took some time to look at the different parts of the Android operating system. We started out with some of the basics of this system before moving on to how set up the architecture that is inside of the code, how to create one of your own programs, and even how to set up an emulator so that you can run the code on your computer (which can be nice if you don't have a specific Android device around) and see how it is going to work for you.

There is so much to love with the Android operating system. With billions of devices around the world using this system for making apps or running the programs that they want on their mobile devices, it is easy to learn how to use this operating system for developing your own apps or for your own personal use. Use this guidebook to learn more about how the Android operating system works and to make it create the best programs for you..